TONIA TODMAN'S
Heirloom Sewing
BOOK

First published in 1992 by
Sally Milner Publishing
558 Darling Street
Rozelle NSW 2039
Australia

Reprinted 1992

© Todman Services Pty Ltd, 1992

Production by Sylvana Scannapiego,
Island Graphics
Design by Gatya Kelly
Layout by Shirley Peters
Photography by Andrew Elton
Illustrations by Angela Downes
Pattern sheet by Leslie Griffith
Typeset by Shirley Peters
Printed in Malaysia by SRM Production Services

National Library of Australia
Cataloguing-in-Publication data:

Todman, Tonia.
    Tonia Todman's heirloom sewing book.

    ISBN 1 86351 095 8

    1. Sewing. 2. Heirlooms. I. Title. II. Title: Heirloom sewing book.

646.2

Contents

Introduction

Something that's been patiently fashioned from finely woven fabric, lavishly embellished with various cotton laces and then perhaps hand embroidered, is attractive to all of us. It speaks volumes about the love and care shown in its making and must, by any standard, spell romance! Many years ago, around the turn of the century, this type of garment or household item was quite ordinary. Hours of patient hand sewing went into even the most everyday garment or piece of household linen. Plain white or cream cotton was the most readily available fabric for women's blouses and undergarments and for children's clothes. Printed fabrics as we know them today were not at all common then.

Much of the stitching of these garments was done by hand. Sewing machines had yet to become an everyday household item, so various stitches and procedures by hand were perfected for the joining of laces and fabrics. With laces being of standard design, these techniques became the rule, and today we can duplicate them using modern sewing machines. If nothing else, the strength of machine sewing should give us beautiful garments that become very long lasting heirlooms!

These machine techniques are easy – even for a beginner. Much of the complexity of dressmaking is missing in heirloom sewing. In this book all the techniques are illustrated and all the projects incorporate one or more of these processes. This way, even your learning steps will produce something precious!

You will find that I've experimented with some of the more frequently used stitching techniques, and I believe I've found some simpler, neater methods. I've also used printed fabrics for some of my projects, and this is a real step away from tradition! However, I'm confident you'll love the results. Don't misunderstand me, for I love white and pastel voiles, and believe they are absolutely right for this type of sewing. I also believe Liberty's Tana Lawns with their small, endearing designs printed on amazingly fine quality fabric are perfect for heirloom sewing, as they seem to be both up-to-date and timeless in their appeal.

Heirloom sewn embellishments can appear as subtle, or as lavish as you wish. Do not fall into the trap of creating something that is too precious to use – or that makes your heart sink at the thought of laundering it! You will find my approach to heirloom sewing fairly pragmatic; I firmly believe we should use the things we love, not store them away to only admire and handle them occasionally. With the sewing techniques given in this book, you will create sturdy heirloom items quickly – so there is no excuse to lock them away!

Don't be afraid to be your own designer; once you know the techniques you can create your own patterns and designs, and go on to produce truly original work. There is a full-sized, clearly marked pattern sheet at the back of the book for all appropriate projects. If you're a beginner, choose one of the simple projects to make first or, as a more experienced heirloom sewer, consider some of my new ideas and methods to complement those you already use. Either way, I hope you continue to enjoy sewing your heirlooms.

Getting started

Fabric preparation

Pre-shrinking

As heirloom sewn items will inevitably be laundered and ironed, you should pre-shrink the fabric before cutting out the pattern pieces.

A gentle handwash in warm water with a minimum of soap flakes is ideal for cottons. Rinse the fabric well and hang it out to dry, arranged in the most undistorted way you can manage. You may iron the fabric while it is slightly damp; this will help the creases disappear more easily. Lightly spray cottons with starch in the final stages of pressing.

Wool fabric can be pre-shrunk by layering it with damp towels. Fold the towels and fabric together and leave overnight, in a basin or perhaps on the edge of your kitchen sink. By the next morning the fabric will have taken up the moisture and shrunk all it's likely to. Hang the fabric out to dry away from direct sunlight. When dry, press with a steam iron.

Pre-shrink silks as you would cottons, but do not wring out the fabric to remove water, as creases caused by this may be difficult to remove when the fabric is dry. I prefer to roll it in an absorbent bath towel to remove excess water prior to hanging it flat, away from direct sunlight, to dry.

Linen is probably the toughest of the natural fibres, and is well able to contend with long term use. Treat linen as you would cotton, but I suggest you wash linen in slightly hotter water. You need a higher heat setting when pressing, and you will certainly find it easier to iron linen while damp. Lightly spray linen with starch in the final pressing.

Straightening fabrics prior to cutting

More often than not, and despite the best intentions and

skills of the person cutting your purchased fabric, your fabric ends will probably need to be straightened. Go to the selvedge (the woven edge either side of your fabric) and snip with scissors where you wish to make the end straight. Draw out a thread and pull it so that it creates a line across the fabric. Cut across this line and you will have an even end from which to start cutting. This step is vitally important, as pattern pieces should be placed accurately on the straight grain (or bias, if so directed) prior to cutting out. Fold the fabric over, matching selvedges and check that the cut end sits straight. If it still does not do this take one side of the fabric in either hand, with hands diagonally opposite, and pull the fabric. Repeat this as often as needed until the ends of the fabric are even. I suggest you press the fabric again after pulling it into shape.

Fabrics for heirloom sewing

The qualities of natural fibres are just right for heirloom sewing. Pure, fine cotton is the most commonly chosen fabric, closely followed by the finer weaves of wool, silk and linen. There is a special look about heirloom sewn garments, and synthetic fabrics don't seem to fit this image. The crispness of a fine cotton blouse or baby's dress, or the soft rustle of a pure silk nightgown can't be found in synthetic fabrics. So, resolve here and now only to purchase the finest natural fabrics. After all, these lovingly sewn items need to last through the generations, and quality fabrics will certainly help you achieve this. The cotton fabric names you will become familiar with are lawn, batiste, and voile.

Laces and Swiss embroidered trims

Swiss embroideries

The term Swiss embroidery refers to any trimming that has a recognisable fabric background. It has an embroidered main panel, and the embroidery often forms a scalloped edge. Sometimes the embroidery is in colours, and can be down the centre of a narrow fabric strip that has two raw side edges. Laces commonly known as broderie anglais are of the Swiss embroidery type. These laces are embroidered on full widths of fabric by highly complex embroidering machines, with row after row of the same lace being embroidered down the length of the fabric, not across. After the embroidery process is finished, the lace is 'cut away' in rows from the fabric by another automatic machine. This is why you sometimes see threads coming from under the scalloped edge, and the remaining raw edge of the lace is cut in the same shape as the scallops.

Types of Swiss embroidery trim

Entredeux

This is the narrow, evenly woven beading that acts as a division between laces, or fabric and laces, or just as a trim linking two sections of an item, for example, between the bodice and the sleeves of a dress, or between the skirt and the hem of a dress. It is woven in different widths and thicknesses, and is best matched to the weight of your fabric and other laces. A band of fine cotton fabric extends from either side of the embroidered beading. Sometimes these bands are cut away during the lace application, or the band may be left on to

Entredeux

fasten the entredeux to fabric or lace. Trimmed entredeux refers to the cutting away of these fine cotton bands, not to any form of embellishment.

Swiss edging

This can be of any width, from very narrow to widths that would almost classify the edging as fabric with one raw edge and the other embroidered and scalloped. They have open, evenly spaced patterns.

Swiss insertion

This has either two woven, straight edges, or one row of entredeux on either side, with bands of fabric extending from these.

Swiss beading

Rows of entredeux are often found on either side. It has embroidered evenly spaced holes through which ribbon may be threaded.

Types of woven lace

Edging lace

These have one straight edge and the other scalloped or similarly shaped. Most edging laces have a strong thread woven into the straight edge, and when this thread is pulled, the lace gathers

Insertion lace

These laces vary in widths and textures. Each side of insertion lace is straight and the pattern of the lace is centred. Most have strong gathering threads woven into each edge.

Beading lace

These are woven with a series of centred holes through which you can thread ribbon. They may also be woven with lace edging combined with the beading. They are not designed to be gathered.

Dyeing laces or Swiss embroideries

It is quite easy to tint white lace to the desired colour by dyeing it with coffee or tea. Coffee gives a pale, yellowed cream colour, whereas tea tinting results in a brown, pale ecru shade. Follow these steps below to test both methods on scrap cotton lace and see which colour you prefer.

- Make a cup of black coffee or tea. Add three dessert-spoons of white vinegar to the mixture and stir. Pour this mixture into a bowl to cool.

- Loosely bundle the lace to be dyed and immerse it into the solution. Leave it only for a few seconds, thoroughly mixing it around in the liquid to be sure all the lace is coloured. Remove the lace, squeeze out liquid and check the colour. If it is too dark, rinse the lace under tepid water until the desired shade is reached. If it is still too dark, rub in some toilet soap to create suds in the lace, then rinse again. If the lace is too light, repeat the dipping process until the desired shade is reached.

- After the lace is tinted, lay it out flat to dry. Do not put it into the tumble dryer as this tends to tangle the lace and make it difficult to iron flat. Allow it to dry naturally, then starch and iron with a steam iron.

Techniques used in heirloom sewing

Starching lace and fabric

It's best to use a pump-action container or be very sure your pressure pack starch is environmentally friendly! Starching lace and fabric will eliminate many difficulties that can result from stitching fine fabrics.

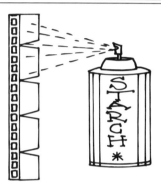

Joining a straight lace edge to a straight lace edge

- Install the machine foot for zigzag stitch and adjust your stitch length to about 1, and the width to just under 2.

- Place the two lace lengths under the machine presser foot and butt the two lengths of lace together, but do not overlap the edges. Adjust the butted edges so that they sit right in the middle of your presser foot.

- Start to zigzag over the two butted edges. Lace edges vary and you will soon find the ideal stitch width and length for the particular laces you are stitching together. You should aim for a discreet stitch, one that does not take in too much of the adjoining lace, and yet still secures the laces together firmly. Do not fall into the trap of making your stitch almost like a satin stitch – this will create unnecessary bulk.

Two straight lace edges joined

- Hold the two laces together as they pass under the machine foot, taking care not to allow either of them to travel at a different pace to the other. Sometimes I find it useful to observe the pattern of the lace and match it from one length to the other. This way I soon see if one length goes out of alignment.

- If joining many rows of insertion lace or beading together, complete your lace panel first before joining it into your garment.

Joining a straight lace edge to fabric

- Place the edge of the lace a little less than 6 mm (¹/₄″) in from the edge of the fabric, with right sides facing. Pin in place if necessary.

- Set your machine to the widest zigzag stitch, with a length of about 1.

- Start zigzagging, being sure that the stitch goes just over the lace heading, and then back right off the edge of the fabric. This wide zigzag stitch has the effect of automatically rolling the fabric edge over towards the lace edge and enclosing it in the stitching, transforming the fabric edge into a small, even roll of fabric which sits at the top of the lace. All raw edge threads disappear and you are left with a very neat, strong finish.

- You will need to stitch a *holding stitch* to flatten the small roll of fabric which forms in the stitching process.

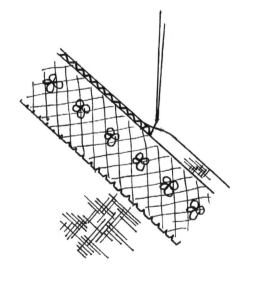

Joining straight lace edge to fabric

Holding stitch

- Turn the lace-trimmed fabric to the right side to have the fabric roll on the wrong side. Adjust your zigzag with length about $1/2$ to 1. Bring your presser foot down directly over the small fabric roll at the back of the lace. Start stitching, making sure the small zigzag is discreet and no wider than it has to be. The purpose of this stitch is to hold the fabric roll flat against the fabric and therefore allow the lace to sit flat. It will also add more strength to this surprisingly sturdy edge treatment. There is another method of holding the lace and fabric in place using the blind hem stitch. These details are given in the technique *Applying entredeux to gathered fabric*.

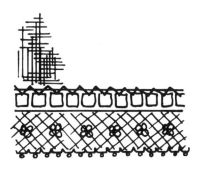

Holding stitch

Joining a straight lace edge to entredeux

- Trim away one woven fabric edge of the entredeux.

- Butt together the straight edge of lace and the cut edge of the entredeux under the sewing machine presser foot.

- Set your machine to a zigzag stitch that is spaced so that the stitches go into each of the spaces in the woven beading of the entredeux. You will find this is difficult, and that the best you may be able to do is to approximate this.

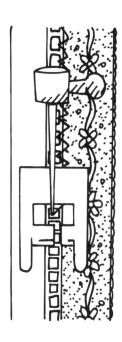

Joining straight lace edge to entredeux

Joining entredeux to flat fabric

Method 1

Method 1

Method 1

- Place entredeux onto fabric with right sides facing and raw edges even.

- Straight stitch in the ditch, or right beside the beading edge. Stitch again 3 mm (1/8″) away in the seam allowance.

- Trim away excess fabric close to the second row of stitching. Stitch a narrow, close zigzag over the second row of stitching.

- Turn the piece to the right side, spray lightly with starch and press, pushing the seam allowance towards the fabric.

- Straight stitch just outside the edge of the entredeux through all thicknesses to hold seam allowance towards the fabric.

Method 2

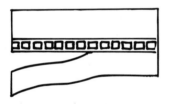

Step 1

Method 2

- Trim away one side of the entredeux.

- Place trimmed edge of entredeux 3 mm (1/8″) in from the edge of the fabric, right sides facing.

- Adjust your machine to a wide zigzag stitch of about width 3, with a length of about 2.

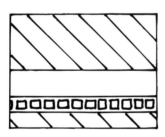

Step 2

- Stitch the entredeux to the fabric, having the stitches go into the beading spaces of the entredeux, and off the edge of the fabric. This will automatically roll the fabric edge inwards, forming a small, tight roll just on the edge of the entredeux.

- Turn the piece to the right side and press. The small roll of fabric will sit facing the entredeux. See *Holding stitch* for the next step.

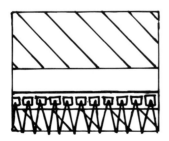

Step 3

Stitching straight edged lace to fabric, then cutting away fabric from beneath

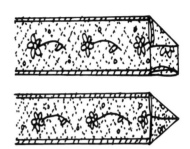

Fold ends to make point

- Place a length of starched insertion or beading on the fabric where you wish to have the trim. If you are catching the ends of the lace into a seam, leave them as they are. If you have the end of the lace in the centre of the fabric, fold under the exposed end 1 cm (1/2″) then fold in the corners to make a point at the end of the lace. Be sure the point is exactly in the centre and the folded angles are even. Pin, then spray with starch.

- Using small, narrow zigzag stitch, oversew lace edges, stitching lace onto the fabric, and being sure to stitch any points very accurately.

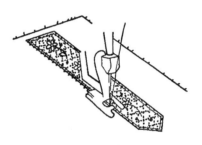

Oversew lace edges

- Using small embroidery scissors, carefully cut away fabric and lace point folds from behind the lace, cutting close to the zigzag stitching. Press again.

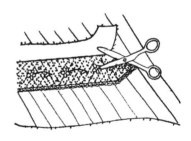

Cut away fabric from behind lace

Gathering lace by hand

All laces with a straight woven edge have a strong, straight thread along the straight edge. When this thread is pulled, the lace gathers, and it is simple to adjust gathers to the required fullness. Using a pin, find this thread and pull it out of the lace near one end; pull it up to gather lace.

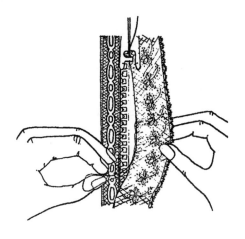

Joining entredeux to hand gathered lace

Joining entredeux to hand gathered lace

- Gather the lace to the correct length using the method described above.

- Trim the fabric edge from one side of the entredeux.

- Place the gathered lace and the trimmed entredeux edge under the presser foot, centred and butted together.

- Adjust your machine to a medium width zigzag, with a medium to short length. The stitch should enclose the gathered edge and swing into the spaces in the entredeux's beading.

- Stitch the two edges together, adjusting the gathers as needed while stitching.

- If stitching gathered trim around a corner, be sure to allow extra gathers at the corner as this will prevent the corner trim rolling under.

Applying entredeux to gathered fabric

- To gather fabric, stitch a row of gathering 6 mm (1/4″) away from the fabric's raw edge, then stitch another row of gathering 6 mm (1/4″) away from the first row.

- Pulling on both the bobbin threads at the same time, draw up the gathering to make the desired amount of fullness.

- With right sides facing and raw edges matching, place the entredeux on to the gathered fabric. Check that the ditch of the entredeux (where the edge of the beading meets the woven fabric edge) sits between the rows of gathering, and adjust if necessary.

- Sew along the ditch of the entredeux with straight stitch.

- Add extra gathers at any corners as this extra full-ness will prevent the fabric rolling under at the corners.

- Stitch again, in the seam allowance, 3 mm (1/8″) from the previous row of stitching.

- Trim excess fabric away close to second row of stitching. Adjust your machine to narrow zigzag and overcast the second row of stitching.

- Turn the piece to the right side and push the seam allowance towards the fabric. If available, adjust your machine to a blind hem stitch. For those unfamiliar with it, the stitch is available on most zigzag machines and comprises four or five straight stitches and then one zigzag to the left. There is no need to install the blind hem foot.

- Place your entredeux under the presser foot, adjusting it so that the needle will stitch a straight stitch in the ditch of the entredeux closest to the gathers, and the zigzag will reach into the gathers enough to secure them. Test this stitch for a short distance, adjusting your machine until the correct width of zigzag is reached. Generally a stitch width of 1½ is adequate. If your machine does not do blind hem stitch, use a narrow zigzag over the edge of the gathers. I prefer the blind hem stitch as it is less obtrusive, however, both stitches will hold the gathers away from the entredeux.

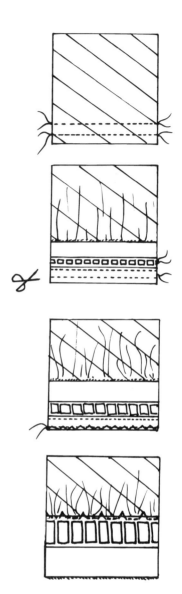

Inserting entredeux into fabric, with hem

- Stitch the side seams of the skirt, or the underarm seam of the sleeve.

- Decide how deep you wish your hem to be, and note that this will dictate where the entredeux will be positioned on the skirt or sleeve. For example, if you want a 7.5 cm (3″) hem, you will need to cut a band off the hem that is 15 cm (6″) wide.

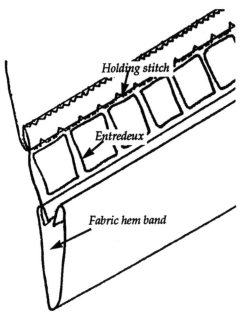

Inserting entredeux into fabric with hem

- Stitch one fabric edge of entredeux to the widest fabric section following the method given for *Joining entredeux to flat fabric: Method 1*, starting at a side seam and overlapping the ends of the entredeux 1 cm (³/₈″).

- Join the upper edge of the hem band to the remaining fabric edge of entredeux, by repeating the previous step, being sure to align the seam with the upper section.

- Press under 6 mm (¹/₄″) on remaining edge of hem band. Trim turned edge neatly to 3 mm (¹/₈″). Bring this folded edge up to the ditch of the entredeux and baste. Press, then hem by hand, using tiny stitches.

Trimming corners with entredeux

- While it is possible to do so, do not try to stitch one continuous strip of entredeux around a 90 degree angle. You will achieve a better result using the following method.

- Assume we are trimming the edge of a square collar. Lay strips of untrimmed entredeux down the sides first and cut off entredeux 1.5 cm (⁵/₈″) beyond collar edge. Stitch in place using method for *Joining entredeux to flat fabric: Method 1*. Turn to right side and press seam towards collar.

- Lay strips of entredeux on remaining straight edges, extending entredeux over those strips already stitched in place. Stitch as before.

- You will now be able to trim away the remaining fabric edge of the entredeux to apply flat or gathered lace. See methods for *Joining entredeux to flat lace or gathered lace*.

Sewing flat lace to a 90 degree corner, and mitring corners

- Zigzag the starched lace to the finished edge – probably entredeux – and stop stitching right at the corner.

- Allow your lace to extend beyond the corner by the same amount as its width. For example, if using a 2 cm (1″) wide lace, the extension will be 2 cm (1″). Fold the lace back against itself, forming a diagonal fold extending out from the fabric corner. Pin, then press.

- Stitch, with narrow zigzag, from the inside corner to the outside corner over the lace fold, securing your threads well. Trim lace away from beneath fold close to stitching.

- Continue zigzagging lace around finished edge.

- If you plan to have several rows of lace joined in a wide trim for an edge that will go around a corner, you may prefer to join all the lace strips first then make one large mitre at the corner, instead of one for each row.

Another method of mitring a 90⁰ corner is to place the lace ends together and stitch at a 45⁰ angle. On the reverse side, trim away the excess lace

Sewing flat lace to an angle that is not 90 degrees

- Zigzag starched lace to fabric edge. This edge could be entredeux or you could be stitching the flat lace to a raw fabric edge with wide zigzag. Stop stitching right at corner. If the fabric is hard to manoeuvre (and it probably will be), take it out from under the presser foot and clip your threads. Start stitching again once you have made your lace angle.

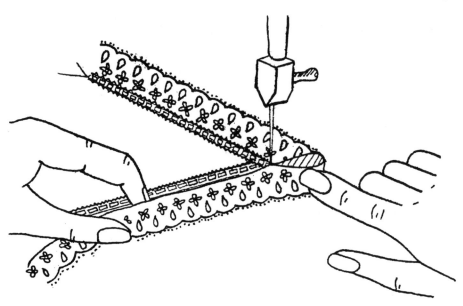

Stitching lace to an angle that is not 90 degrees. Note the overlapped entredeux

- Working from the right side, fold lace into an angle that gives a correct line from the point of the fabric to the edge of the lace, and still allows the lace to be in the correct position to continue stitching after the angle. There is no mathematical theory to this method – use a visual estimate and adjust until it looks right. Once you are satisfied with the angle, pin through the fold.

- Fold the lace back to continue stitching if you are attaching it to a raw edge, or butt it to the edge of the previous row of lace or entredeux. Continue stitching lace to finished edge.

- zigzag finely over the fold in the angle and cut away excess lace from behind the stitching.

Finishing a neckline with entredeux and gathered lace

- If using a commercial pattern where the seam allowances are 1.5 cm ($^5/_8''$), trim the seam allowance around the neckline to be equal to the width of the fabric extension at the side of entredeux.

- Clip through fabric extensions of untrimmed entredeux to edge of embroidered beading every 1cm ($^1/_2''$), or less, to allow for easing.

- Pin the entredeux around the neckline (allowing sufficient for back opening turnbacks), having right sides facing and raw edges matching. Stitch in the ditch of the entredeux using straight stitching.

- Stitch again 3 mm ($^1/_8''$) away in the seam allowance. Trim close to second row of stitching and narrow zigzag over this edge. Clip seam allowance to edge of entredeux taking care not to clip stitching.

- Turn piece to right side, press seam allowance towards fabric. Trim remaining edge from entredeux.

- Apply gathered lace to trimmed edge of entredeux following instructions for *Joining entredeux to gathered lace.*

- Place the edge of another row of gathered lace in the ditch of the entredeux nearest the dress fabric and fasten it using the method above, stitching through all thicknesses. This will provide a pretty neckline or sleeve edge trim that will also hold down the seam allowance.

Step 1. Wrong side of garment. The lower row of gathered lace is already in place
Step 2. Finished neckline

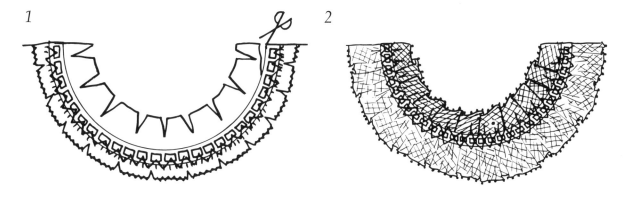

1   2

Seam finishes

There are only two seam finishes that are appropriate for fine, sheer fabrics. Both are correct, so choose the method you prefer.

French seams

This traditional technique evolved because a firm and comfortable seam finish was required for underclothes. It is still widely used in clothing, as it completely encloses the raw fabric edge and leaves a soft fabric-only seam allowance.

- Note that French seams take up an allowance of 1.2 cm ($^1/_2''$) only, and you should adjust your seam allowance if using a commercial pattern.

- With wrong sides facing and raw edges matching, stitch 6 mm ($^1/_4''$) from the raw edges. Trim these edges to a little less than 3 mm ($^1/_8''$).

- Turn the piece to the wrong side and press the seam flat, taking care to have the seam line accurately placed on the folded edge. You now have right sides of fabric facing.

- Stitch again, 6 mm ($^1/_4''$) from folded edge, enclosing previous seam allowance. Turn to right side and press seam allowance to one side.

French seam

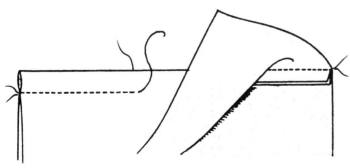

Seam with narrow allowance and overcast edges

- Place fabric pieces together with right sides facing and raw edges matching. Stitch along seam line. Stitch again 3 mm ($^1/_8$") away.

- Trim seam allowance close to the second row of stitching.

- Adjust your machine to a very narrow, medium length zigzag stitch and overcast this second row of stitching.

Seam with narrow allowance and overcast edges

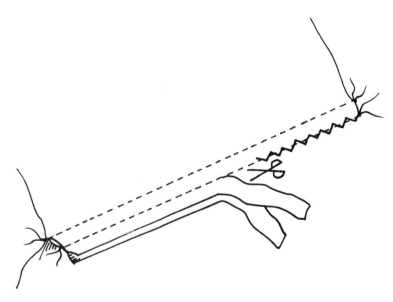

Continuous bands

Continuous bands provide an efficient, neat way of finishing a garment opening. Self fabric is used, ideally starched before use.

- Check that the length of your cut band is sufficiently long to stitch around to both sides of the opening split.

- Press under 1 cm (1/2″) on one long edge of band then trim pressed turn under away to 6 mm (1/4″) for neatness.

- Spread split edges apart. Baste the right side of the continuous band's unpressed edge to the right side of the opening edge. See the illustration for positioning details, noting that the seam allowance of the split in fact comes down to the bare minimum at the pivot point. Stitch in place.

- Press the seam allowance towards the band, then bring the pressed edge over and align it with the stitching. Press it into place. Hand sew pressed edge to stitching.

Attaching a continuous band

Tips for tucks

Twin needle tucks

Twin needles make the easiest pin tucks I know! Most machines will sew with these needles, and the time they save is wonderful. Fit the pintuck foot to your machine. This foot has a number of grooves in the base of its plate through which the stitched tucks pass. It is helpful for aligning close tucks as the previously sewn row passes through the adjoining groove. Thread your machine with two strands of thread, taking one either side of the tension gauge, if possible, to avoid twisted threads. Using your quilter's guide, or the side of your presser foot for closer tucks, simply stitch rows with the twin needle. Two parallel rows of stitching appear, with the bobbin thread pulling slightly underneath which causes the fabric between the stitching to be slightly raised, creating the tuck. There are various widths of twin needle available, so choose whichever size suits your purpose.

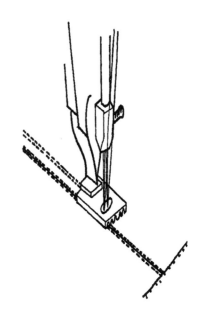

Twin needle tucks

Traditional tucks

This classic trim tends to worry sewers – getting tucks to be straight is the main problem! As tucks are always sewn on the straight grain of the fabric I like to draw out threads where the stitching lines will be. Fold in the tuck; by bringing these lines together you have a perfectly straight, accurately spaced tuck. As the fabrics you are working with are finely woven, the drawing out of threads will not be noticed. Stitch down the drawn thread line, making your tuck and concealing the space where the thread was.

When making a tucked sleeve, collar or yoke, or any other section that is largely tucked, make your tucked fabric first. Spray the fabric with starch and press the

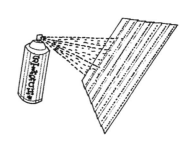

Spray with starch

tucks well, then cut out your pattern piece.

When stitching a group or panel of tucks, I prefer to stitch tucks all in the one direction, that is, I always start stitching from the same end. I find that this prevents a wave effect showing in the tucked panel. Don't overlook using tucks on an angle. Follow the advice above and make your tucked fabric, then spray with starch and press well. Place your pattern piece onto the tucked fabric so that the tucks sit diagonally, then cut out. If you need two identical pieces, use the first piece cut as a pattern for the second. This effect is particularly appealing on yokes and collars, or as shaped panels set amongst lace borders.

Traditional tucks drying after starching and pressing

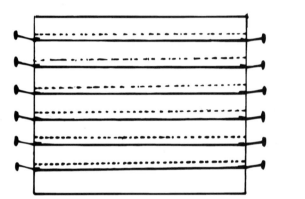

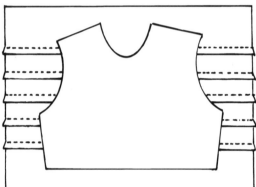

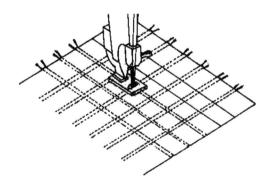

Crisscross or waffle tucks are done with a twin needle

Crisscross, or waffle tucks

This is a simple technique that gives you a wonderful effect. Stitch your tucks in one direction first, then, with the same spacing, stitch again, only this time from a 90 degree angle. The finished effect will be tiny squares all over your work. Use this effect in skirt panels, in yokes and collars. This is a lovely, traditional effect that is inexpensive to create. I suggest you make your fabric first, then cut out your pattern pieces.

Create your own Swiss embroideries

Most machines today do at least a few fancy stitches. It is not difficult to use this facility to create lengths of pretty embroidery to be inserted into your heirloom sewing. Practise first, seeing what designs are appropriate, and use different coloured threads to create a true embroidery effect. The gradually shaded machine embroidery threads are wonderful for this, giving you a truly professional result. One of the major advantages of making your own embroidered strips is that the background fabric can be the same as that of the dress. This will give the item a truly traditional effect, and avoid any badly matched fabrics.

There are many positions on a garment or household linen that lend themselves to being trimmed with an embroidered strip. Try using them around the edge of a collar, or on neck, sleeve and waist bands, set them into fancy hem bands, use them vertically in yokes or set into the fabric of sleeves in strips, across pockets, or between strips of puffing or pintucks. You'll find it only a short time before your embroidered strips resemble true Swiss embroideries!

Lace applique

The exquisite trim so often seen on expensive underwear and nightwear is appliqued lace. This, I'll admit, looks complex and time consuming! Well, that impression is partially correct, but it is not difficult. The secret lies in choosing laces that lend themselves to applique, and becoming adept at using narrow, fine zigzag stitch accurately. This trimming looks luxurious when used generously on nightgowns, perhaps around a neckline or hem or sleeves. Choose wide cotton laces, or finely woven polyester blends of around 7 cm wide (3") or a little more. Refer to the illustration for this technique, for it is important that you understand the sequence of stitching then cutting away fabric and lace to finish the work.

Cutting away the fabric from behind the appliqued lace

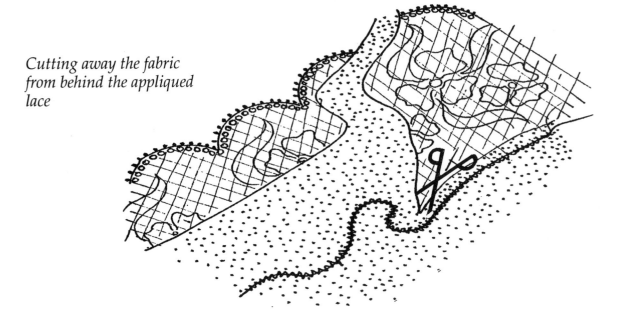

- Select a lace with a pattern edge that can be easily distinguished, as it is around the edge of this pattern that you stitch. Find laces with a solid, continuous pattern, as patterns with wide channels of tulle are ineffective.

- Ascertain the right side of your lace – it is usually more textured and the edges of motifs may be lightly corded, and therefore, raised.

- Always stitch with thread the same colour as the lace.

- Pin your lace around the edge to be trimmed, having the scalloped edge of the lace on the outside and the right side upwards and overlapping the cut ends by a measurement equal to the width of the lace. If you are pinning lace to a bias – cut edge, take care not to stretch the fabric, or if in doubt work with a long length of lace and only cut when you approach the overlapping finishing point.

- Turn your machine to a narrow zigzag stitch. This is important, as the stitch should be unobtrusive, yet close and wide enough to hold the lace securely. Take a good look at the pattern repeats in your lace, and especially the edge of the pattern. Start stitching over this pattern edge, so that the stitch completely covers the edge of the design. Take your time stitching, and turn corners neatly, leaving your needle down in the work as you turn. Do take the trouble to go around and into all the curves and indentations in the pattern edge, for it is this complex outline that makes the technique so attractive.

- When stitching is nearly complete and you are about 10 cm (4″) from the overlap, stop stitching and clip the threads. Remove the item from under the machine presser foot. Place the overlap area flat and adjust it until the pattern on both layers of lace seems to have a logical stitching line through it. It would be a great coincidence for the pattern to match accurately! You should look to have the outside edge level, and be able to see a stitching line that flows through the lace pattern from the outside edge to the opposite edge. Pin, or baste, the overlapped lace ends together. Push the fabric away from under the lace and then zigzag through the lace to join the ends, following your planned stitching line. Be sure to stitch the outside edge securely, as this area usually takes strain during wearing.

- Using small, sharp scissors, cut away the excess overlap on the top and lower laces, cutting close to the stitching. Be very careful doing this, and pin through the overlap to identify it to avoid cutting on the wrong side of the stitching, which would be a real calamity!

- Re-pin the joined lace to the fabric and continue stitching around the pattern outline until completed.

- Start carefully cutting away the lace close to the stitching on the right side, taking care to remove all obvious threads and sections of lace.

- Turn your work over and cut away the fabric from under the lace, leaving no more than 6 mm (1/4″) fabric allowance from the stitching.

- When peaks or concave angles are part of your edges to be trimmed, as in the case of a camisole top, the same methods for overlapping ends of lace apply, except you are working with a continuous piece of lace. Stop stitching short of the angle and fold your lace to have an overlap that creates the correct angle. Adjust the overlapped patterns to find a stitching line. When the angle is pinned in place you will see where you can cut through the lace to allow both edges to sit flat and overlap, allowing for a clear stitching line. I do not like cutting through the woven outside edge unless absolutely necessary, so when cutting through the lace stop just short of the edge and then overlap. The small section of the woven edge that remains uncut will sit quite flat enough. Push the fabric away from the back of the overlap and zigzag through the lace stitching line. Trim away the excess lace close to the stitching line from on top and underneath, taking great care to cut away the correct pieces.

- Re-pin the joined lace to the fabric and continue to finish stitching around the pattern outline, then trim away lace and fabric as instructed. Treat all angles in the same way, adjusting the folded lace to sit well into the angle.

Duck billed scissors are designed to keep lace away from the cutting edge

Beautiful bed linen

Silk taffeta sachets

Lace appliqué sleep pillow, sachet and coathanger

Detail of the stitching technique

Lace appliqué camisole and knickers

Kate's christening gown

Detail of lace at hem

Alice's dress

Phoebe's Liberty dress and pinafore

Phoebe's pink voile dress

Lucy the heirloom doll

Heirloom treasures

These pretty essentials would be welcome in any trousseau, but by making them yourself, you can afford to rate them as everyday indispensables!

Trimmed heirloom sheets

There is much scope here for trimming the turn-back edge of sheets of any size. You may well already have the sheets, or you may be able to purchase good quality white sheeting by the metre and make your sheets. While I've used Swiss embroidered lace, you could easily substitute an insertion lace that was crochet-like in its appearance. The insertion I used has entredeux edges woven into it. If your insertion comes without entredeux, add rows of entredeux either side of your lace, following the technique *Joining a straight lace edge to entredeux*. Instructions given below assume purchased sheets have no decorative fold-back panel on top edge.

MATERIALS

- Sheet in your choice of size, or sheeting fabric cut to size

- Insertion lace for turn-back trim

- Twin needle

METHOD

- Cut off approximately 30 cm (12") from one end of the sheet, drawing a thread, if necessary, to be sure you cut accurately.

- Stitch a length of insertion to the larger piece of sheeting, following the technique *Joining entredeux to flat fabric: Method 2*. Stitch a holding stitch, also, as suggested in the *Joining a straight lace edge to fabric* instructions.

- Press under 1 cm (1/2") on one long edge of the remaining piece of sheeting. Trim this fold-under to 6 mm (1/4"). Stitch the unfolded raw sheeting edge to the remaining edge of the insertion lace, following the technique *Joining entredeux to flat fabric: Method 2*, placing instead the fabric's right side against the wrong side of the entredeux edging. Do not stitch a holding stitch.

- Bring the 6 mm (1/4") folded edge over to the right side and align it with the stitched edge of entredeux, so that the fold sits in the ditch of the entredeux and the roll of fabric underneath faces the sheeting. Turn your machine to a narrow zigzag and stitch this folded edge in place. This will also act as a holding stitch. You now have a double, folded edge on the sheet.

- Make several rows of twin needle tucks on the main body of the sheet just in from the insertion trim, and finish with one row of small wave stitch (if available on your machine) still using your twin needle.

- If you have made the sheets yourself, finish the sides and lower edge with 2 cm (1") hems.

Trimmed heirloom pillowcase

MATERIALS

- Sheeting fabric (see below)
- 1.70 m (70") of wide Swiss embroidered insertion lace
- 4.80 m (192") of wide Swiss embroidered edging lace
- Twin needle

METHOD

- 1 cm ($1/2$″) seams allowed.

- Cut one piece of sheeting 50 x 70 cm (20″ x 28″), and another 50 x 72 cm (20″ x 29″). Cut another piece 50 x 20 cm for pillow shield, and a frill strip 4.80 m x 6 cm (192″ x $2^1/2$″).

- Join frill strips, if necessary, using French seams.

- Place the edging against the frill strip, right sides facing, and having the edge of the lace 3 mm ($1/8$″) in from the fabric edge. Turn your machine to a wide, close zigzag and stitch over the raw edges. The stitching will roll the raw edges inwards and contain them. Turn work to the right side and sew, using the technique described in *Holding stitch.*

- Using the twin needle, make a small wave stitch below the lace stitching line.

- Press a crease around the 50 x 70 cm (20″ x 28″) piece that is 12 cm (5″) in from the edges. This crease will give you a stitching line to follow for the outer edge of the insertion lace.

- Stitch the insertion to the sheeting using a small, narrow zigzag and mitring the corners. Make several rows of twin needle tucks around the insertion lace, finishing the outer edges of tucks with rows of small wave stitch, still using the twin needle.

- Gather the frill strip and apply, right sides facing, to the trimmed piece of sheeting. Allow extra gathers for fullness at the corners to ensure the frill sits straight, rather than rolling under.

- Fold over one 50 cm (20″) wide end of the remaining sheeting piece 1 cm ($1/2$″), then again 2 cm (1″), and stitch. Place the hemmed back piece over the trimmed piece, right sides together and with frill facing the centre. Position the hemmed edge level with the frill stitching. Stitch down sides and across short raw end. Leave pillowcase flat, with hemmed back piece uppermost.

- On one 50 cm (20″) edge of the pillow shield piece turn under 1 cm ($1/2$″), and then 2 cm (1″), and stitch. Place the shield piece over the hemmed back piece, matching the raw edges. Stitch short edges of shield, following previous stitching, and across side edge of pillowcase, stitching over the frill stitching, and taking care not to catch the hemmed top of the back piece in the stitching.

Old-fashioned heirloom pillowcase with ties

MATERIALS

- One piece of sheeting 1 m x 70 cm (39" x 28")
- Four pieces sheeting, each 30 x 10 cm (12" x 4") for ties
- 2 m (78") wide entredeux
- 1 m (39") Swiss embroidered edging

METHOD

- Cut two 2 cm (1") wide strips from one 1 m (39")wide edge of the sheeting.
- Stitch entredeux to one 1 m (39") edge of the sheeting, following technique for *Joining entredeux to flat fabric: Method 1* and *Holding stitch*.
- Join one fabric strip to the remaining entredeux edge, then follow with another row of entredeux, then the last fabric strip, using the same sewing techniques.
- Trim the raw edge of the Swiss embroidered edging straight, if necessary. Attach it to the entredeux, following the technique *Joining entredeux to flat fabric: Method 2*. Follow with the technique *Holding stitch*.
- Fold ties over in half lengthways, right sides facing. Trim one end of each tie on an angle. Stitch down the long sides and across angled ends. Turn ties to right sides, turning in the raw, open ends 1 cm ($^1/_2$"). Press, being sure that the creases are accurate.
- Fold the trimmed piece to have the 70 cm (28") sides together and join them with a French seam. Press the pillowcase flat. Stitch across the untrimmed end using a French seam.

- On the open end place the ties 15 cm (6") in from either side of the pillowcase and on both the front and the back. Pin, then stitch in an oblong near the inner row of stitching that holds the entredeux trim in place.

- Place a pillow into the pillowcase, then tie the ties into bows to hold it.

Lace appliqued coathanger

Pretty coathangers are always welcome as a present; and what woman would not like the luxury of a wardrobe full of padded coathangers! Wooden hangers are usually available in packs from chain stores, and are really an inexpensive start to a beautiful and useful item. I like to rub some perfumed oil into the wooden hanger prior to covering it. Lavender oil is good, as it is enduring, a proven moth-chaser and helps to prevent mustiness in your cupboard.

MATERIALS

- Strips of polyester wadding to pad the hanger

- Wooden hanger with hook

- Bias strip of fabric 4 cm x 20 cm (1$\frac{1}{2}$" x 8") to cover hook

- Fabric strip 20 cm (8") wide and twice the length of the hanger

- Lace, suitable for applique, of the same length as the fabric strip

- Fabric strip 35 x 7.5 cm (14" x 3") for bow

METHOD

To pad hanger

Wind the strips of polyester wadding around the wooden hanger until all wood is covered. Take care to cover the ends and to distribute padding evenly. Two or three layers of strips are needed to achieve a well padded hanger. Pull the strips firmly as you wind, stitching

ends to secure. Relocate the drilled hole for the hook and screw in hook.

To cover hook

Fold bias strip in half, right sides facing and edges matching. Stitch 6 to 7 mm (1/4″) from fold, then stitch again 7 to 8 mm (3/8″) from fold. Cut off excess fabric close to second row of stitches. Turn bias to right side, slide over hook. Tuck top raw end inside, hand stitch end to secure. Pull down bias firmly, trimming away any excess. Hand stitch bias firmly to wadding near neck of hook.

METHOD

- Applique the lace to one long edge of the fabric strip (this will be the bottom edge of the cover), following the technique in *Lace applique.*

- Bring the short ends of the strip together, wrong sides facing, and stitch a French seam. With right sides facing and seam at one end, stitch upper edges together in a 1 cm (1/2″) seam, leaving a gap at centre for hook. Turn to right side and mark hanger gap with a pin, then fold and press upper seam edge accurately.

- Make a gathering stitch along the upper edge through all thicknesses, 8 mm (3/8″) from the fold, leaving a gap in the centre at pin for hook. Slip cover over hanger and pin lower edges together. Stitch using gathering stitch just below bottom edge of hanger. This may sound difficult, but you do not have to stitch close to the hanger and there is room for your machine foot. Stitch right across above lace, through all thicknesses.

- Draw up top and bottom gathering threads adjusting gathers evenly. Thread gathering threads onto a needle then stitch with them to secure gathers. Fasten off securely.

- Fold bow strip in half lengthways, right sides facing. Trim ends to an angle. Stitch around all open sides, leaving a small gap in centre for turning. Turn out, pulling out points carefully, then press seam accurately. Tie around base of hook into a bow.

Floral sachet with lace applique

MATERIALS

- 1 piece Tana Lawn 36 x 24 cm (14" x 9½")

- 1 length each of insertion lace and applique lace 38 cm (15") long

- Small piece of tulle (optional)

- Ribbon, or a self fabric tie to close

- Potpourri to fill finished sachet

METHOD

- Applique lace across one 36 cm (14") edge as instructed in the technique *Lace applique.*

- Apply the strip of insertion across the remaining 36 cm (14") edge, having the lower edge of the lace 2 cm (1") from the edge as instructed in the technique *Stitching straight edged lace to fabric, then cutting away the fabric from beneath.* Line the lace first with tulle if it is likely to allow potpourri to escape, then treat this as one layer.

- Fold the trimmed piece, right sides out, to have the 24 cm (9½") edges meeting and sew a French seam along side edge and across bottom edges. Press neatly and fill with potpourri. Tie a self fabric tie or ribbon around to close the sachet. The lace will allow the scent of the potpourri to escape.

Silk taffeta padded sachet

MATERIALS

- Two pieces of taffeta 33 x 60 cm (13" x 24")

- Thin wadding, same size as above

- Four triangular pieces of taffeta 18 x 18 cm x 12 cm (7" x 7" x 4½")

- Approximately 2 m (80") of self fabric piping

- One strip of taffeta 115 x 12 cm (45 " x 5") for decorative tie

- One strip of taffeta 35 x 15 cm (14" x 6") for tucked band

- Two strips each of insertion lace and entredeux 35 cm (14") long

- Twin needle

METHOD

- In the centre of the 35 cm (14") wide strip of fabric, make 8 rows of twin needle stitching as a base for waffle tucks; complete following the technique *Waffle tucks*. Spray completed tucks with starch and pin flat on ironing board to dry, then press. Stitch trimmed entredeux to edges of lace by using *Joining a straight lace edge to entredeux*. Stitch a lace strip to each long edge of tucked fabric by butting trimmed entredeux edges up to outside tucks and zigzagging over edges of entredeux, trying not to stitch over tucks. Trim away excess taffeta from underneath lace. Spray with starch and press to stabilise.

- Place lace-trimmed strip over and across one end of one taffeta strip, approximately 5 cm (2") in from the end. zigzag the entredeux edges to the taffeta. Round off the corners nearest the lace trim using a tumbler as a guide. Also round off two corners of one narrow end of the remaining taffeta piece.

- Pin, then stitch piping around the edges of the trimmed taffeta piece, taking a 1 cm (½") seam allowance. Clip seam allowance at corners for ease.

- Place the untrimmed taffeta piece over the trimmed piece, right sides facing. Place the layer of wadding onto these. Pin through all thicknesses. Stitch around, following stitching for piping, leaving a gap for turning at straight short end. Trim wadding close to stitching, then turn sachet to right side. Close opening with tiny hand stitches into the piping stitching.

- Place triangles together in pairs with right sides facing, and round off the angle where the 18 cm (7″) sides meet. Taking a 1 cm (¹/₂″) seam, stitch around, leaving an opening for turning on one 18 cm (7″) side. Turn, press accurately.

- Align one pointed corner of a triangle with the pointed corner of the sachet, tucking the triangle in behind the piping. Taking tiny hand stitches into the piping stitching, stitch the edge of the triangles to the sachet until you reach the other pointed corner of the triangle. These triangles form the sachet gussets and the rounded corner becomes the base of the bag.

- Fold the tie strip in half lengthways, and press an 8 cm (3″) long crease in the fold at each end. Cut the ends into an angle, sloping down from the fold. Using this crease as a pivoting point and leaving your needles down in the fabric while turning, make rows of twin needle pintucks over the ends of the tie. Fold trimmed tie to have right sides facing and stitch around raw edges, leaving an opening for turning. Turn out, press edges accurately and then starch.

- Place the tie around the sachet and tie into a bow to sit just below the trimmed panel. Catch stitch the tie to sachet base with concealed hand stitches.

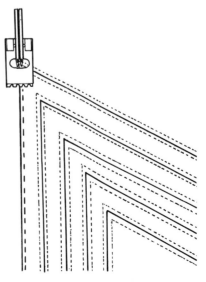

Pivoting while stitching twin needle pin tucks

Small potpourri-filled taffeta sachet

MATERIALS

- One piece of taffeta 30 x 30 cm (12" x 12")
- 30 cm (12") insertion lace
- Small piece of tulle
- 60 cm (24") entredeux
- Taffeta strip 12 x 70cm (5" x 27") for decorative tie
- Twin needle
- Potpourri

METHOD

- Cut a 5 cm (2") strip from one side of the taffeta piece to allow for lace insertion.

- Line your insertion lace with tulle if it is likely to allow potpourri to fall out, then treat it as one layer.

- Join trimmed entredeux to both sides of the insertion lace, using the technique *Joining a straight lace edge to entredeux*. Press 1 cm ($^1/_2$") under on one 30 cm (12") edge of each taffeta piece then trim to 6 mm ($^1/_4$"). Butt these folded edges to either side of the trimmed lace and narrow zigzag over the edge of the entredeux and the folded fabric.

- Make three rows of twin needle tucks either side of the lace insert.

- Make 5 more tucks 11 cm ($4^1/_2$") up from the tucks at the top of the insertion. Fold the trimmed piece over, matching the ends of the insertion and tucks, with the right sides facing, then stitch down the long side and across the lower edge in a 1 cm ($^1/_2$") seam. Turn to the right side.

- Fold sachet top to the inside at the middle tuck. Make the decorative tie using the same method given in the Silk Taffeta Sachet. Fill the sachet with potpourri and close with the self fabric tie.

Frilled herbal sleep pillow

MATERIALS

- Two pieces of Liberty Tana Lawn 30 cm square (12") and one square of tulle (optional)

- 85 cm (34") of wide insertion lace

- Four fabric strips each 60 x 16 cm (24"x 6$\frac{1}{2}$")

- Potpourri combining sleep-inducing herbs and flowers such as hops, lavender, roses, chamomile and lemon verbena

METHOD

- Fold each strip in half lengthways and mark points on the long raw edges 8 cm (3") from each end. Cut from this point up to the top of the fold on each strip, creating an angled end. Open out strips and place two strips flat together, right sides facing and raw edges matching at one end. Stitch ends taking a 1 cm ($\frac{1}{2}$") seam, beginning and finishing stitching 1 cm from each raw edge. Continue to stitch ends of strips together until they are joined in a continuous square. Turn angled ends to the right side and press the strips in half neatly. Gather along raw edges, but not into the corners.

- Fold and pin insertion lace into a square in the centre of one floral fabric square, forming mitred corners. When satisfied with position and accuracy, press in mitres. Using a tiny zigzag, stitch over the edge of the lace to secure, then cut away fabric from underneath lace, following the technique *Stitching straight edged lace to fabric then cutting away fabric from beneath.* To prevent potpourri falling out, centre tulle square under lace section and pin. Using straight stitch, stitch in the tulle square, stitching close to zigzag stitch. Trim away excess tulle.

- Pin gathered edges of frills to right side of lace-trimmed pillow front, placing corners of frill and front together, and matching raw edges, then stitch in place with a 1 cm ($\frac{1}{2}$") seam. The inner edges of the corners will open 1 cm ($\frac{1}{2}$") where they were left

unstitched, to give you some ease as you stitch the corners.

- Fold the frill out of the way into the centre of the trimmed front, and place the remaining floral square over it, right sides facing. Stitch around, following stitching for frill, and leaving an opening for turning. Turn pillow to right side, fill with herbs and stitch the opening closed by hand.

Camisole and knickers
See pattern outline on pattern sheet

MATERIALS

- 2·1 m (2¼ yds) of 115 cm (45″) fabric
- 4·20 m (4¼ yds) of wide, flat lace suitable for applique
- Narrow elastic to fit waist

METHOD

- Trace off pieces from pattern sheet. The size given is medium – 12-14. You need one front, one back for camisole, and two fronts and two backs for knickers. Note that the camisole pattern is given as below hip length – adjust this before cutting if necessary. Be sure to compare measurements, noting that there should be a loose fit, and that bias-cut fabric tends to cling. Increase or decrease sizes on the side seams if necessary. Fabric cut on the bias should not over-hang the table during the cutting out process, as this will distort it. Read the technique *Lace Applique* before sewing.

- Stitch camisole side seams together using your chosen method. Pin the starched lace around the upper and lower edges having the main scalloped edge on the outside, folding at angles, and starting and finishing at a side seam. Be sure that you have sufficient fabric under your lace; check the stitching line in the lace; be sure that fabric is under each part. Turn your machine to a fine zigzag and start to stitch on the lace, following the pattern in the lace. Zigzag in a line down and over the fold in the lace at angles, then continue stitching around the pattern outline.

- When completely stitched, using small sharp scissors cut away excess lace close to the stitching on the right side, and cut away excess fabric on the wrong side, 6 mm (¹/₄″) from stitching. At angles, cut away excess lace on both sides, leaving only the thin joining line of zigzag stitching.

- Make fine bias–cut rouleau shoulder straps, or use narrow satin ribbon, and attach by hand, or use narrow satin stitch by machine.

- Sew knicker fronts to backs at side seams using the same seam method used for the camisole. Stitch fronts and backs together at centre front and centre back. Apply lace around legs as for camisole, starting and ending at inside leg edges. Cut away lace as instructed earlier. Stitch inside leg seams. Fold over 6 mm (¹/₄″) then 1 cm (¹/₂″) on upper edge of knickers, and stitch, leaving opening for elastic. Insert elastic, adjust for fit, overlap ends and stitch together securely. Stitch opening closed.

Kate's christening gown

See pattern outline on pattern sheet

See pattern outline on pattern sheet

MATERIALS

- 1.60 m (65″) of 115 cm (45″) wide voile

- Narrow Swiss insertion and lace insertion for front yoke

- Entredeux

- Wide insertion lace for hem trim

- Wide edging lace for lower edge of skirt and sleeves

- Press studs or flat buttons for back closure

- Narrow silk ribbon for yoke bows

Finishing a neckline with self-fabric bias binding

Step 1

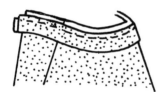

Step 2

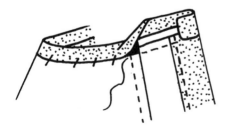

Step 3

METHOD

- Cutting instructions: Cut out the back yokes and sleeves from voile as directed on the pattern sheet. Using the technique *Joining straight edged lace to straight edged lace*, join rows of each narrow insertion alternatively to make a panel of fabric large enough to cut out the front yoke. Cut the front and back skirts, each the full width of fabric and approximately 60 cm (24″) long. Cut away the armholes using the guide. Cut a strip of fabric 22 x 5 cm (9″ x 2″) for continuous band. Cut a 2 cm (1″) wide strip of bias fabric for neckline binding.

- Join the two skirt panels using French seams. Make a split 10 cm (4″) long at the centre of top edge of one skirt panel. Apply a continuous band using the technique *Continuous Bands*. This will be the back skirt.

- Join front and back yokes together at shoulders using French seams. Staystitch the neckline.

- Stitch entredeux to the lower edge of the front and back yokes using the technique *Joining entredeux to flat fabric: Method 2*. Do not trim remaining entredeux edge. Stitch entredeux around armholes using the same technique.

- Bind the neckline to facing edges, finishing the binding by hand.

- Gather the lower sleeve edges to be 16 cm (6″) wide. Apply entredeux to edge, following technique *Applying entredeux to gathered fabric*

- Hand gather wide edging and apply to sleeve entredeux, following technique *Joining entredeux to hand gathered lace.* Join sleeve underarms with French seams.

- Gather across top edges of front and back skirts. Stitch to yokes, following the technique *Applying entredeux to gathered fabric*, folding the back facings to the outside over the skirts as you stitch (see illustration in *Continuous bands*).

- Gather sleeve cap, and stitch into armhole, following the same technique used for sleeve edge.

- With the side seams at the sides, fold the skirt in half, then half again. Measure up the folds 8 cm (3″) and draw a line from this point down to the centre of the raw edges. Cut along these lines, giving you a zigzagged hemline with eight points each at front and back.

- Draw up from the inner points and down to the next, creating a diamond shape. Pin a row of insertion lace 1 cm (¹/₂″) from the raw edges, mitring at angles, and taking it up to the point of the next diamond. Note that only every second point will be pinned. Stitch this to fabric, following technique *Stitching straight edged lace to fabric then cutting away fabric from beneath*. Pin then stitch the overlapping row of insertion lace to the hem, completing the diamonds. Cut away fabric from underneath lace, and from hem edge, close to stitching.

- Stitch entredeux to outer edge of insertion, using technique *Joining a straight lace edge to entredeux.* Trim remaining edge of entredeux and apply hand gathered edging lace, using technique *Joining entredeux to hand gathered lace.*

- Stitch on press studs or make buttonholes and stitch on buttons to back facings to correspond.

- Thread narrow silk ribbon through yoke entredeux and tie into bows.

Petticoat for christening gown
Pattern outlines on pattern sheet

METHOD

- Cut out one front and one back, lengthening them to match christening gown.

- Cut 3 cm (1½″) wide strips of bias fabric to bind neck and armholes.

- Place the front and backs together, wrong sides facing, and stitch French seams at the sides.

- Turn in 6 mm (¼″) raw edges of petticoat shoulders, then turn again at markings and stitch across. Bind neckline and armholes with bias fabric.

- Make buttonholes on front shoulder extensions and sew on buttons in position on back extensions. Trim lower edge of petticoat as desired.

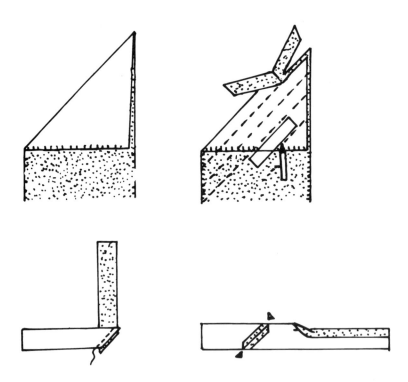

How to cut and join bias binding

Two classic dresses, and a pinafore

The patterns for these garments are shown on the pattern sheet. They are extremely adaptable patterns, and lend themselves to a myriad of different heirloom sewing techniques. The pink dress, Phoebe, shown in sizes 2 years through to 6 years is a traditional European style child's dress. The white dress, Alice, size 4 – 5 years, is more Edwardian in style, with its dropped waist, long full sleeves and pretty collar. The pinafore, also in sizes 2 years to 6 years, is shown over a floral version of 'Phoebe'.

In each case no exact measurements are given for trimming. I give instructions for lace placement for the dresses as they are shown, but I encourage you to design for yourself! You should measure the pattern first to check the size, then calculate amounts of lace and ribbon, considering the effects the width of lace you choose to work with will have on fabric requirements.

Phoebe (Pink voile and lace version)
See pattern outline on pattern sheet

These amounts of fabric allow for a longer skirt than usual. Check the given amounts against your child's measurements before purchasing.

MATERIALS

- 115 cm (45″) wide fabric:

    Size 2: 1.9 m (2 yds)

    Size 3: 2 m (2$^1/_8$y ds)

    Size 4: 2.1 m (2$^1/_4$ yds)

    Size 5: 2.4 m (2$^5/_8$ yds)

    Size 6: 2.6 m (2$^3/_4$ yds)

- Four buttons for back closure, and two for cuffs of long sleeves

- Laces and ribbons as necessary

- Twin needle

METHOD

- Please check the total of the depths of the skirt and the frill measurements given against your child. Bear in mind that the lacy skirt band shown is approximately 6 cm (2$\frac{1}{2}$″) wide and that this affects the length of the skirt. Consider the widths of your lace when calculating skirt length. Whenever you have completed sewing a panel of beading lace, thread ribbon through the lace before joining that panel elsewhere.

- Cut out two skirt panels to the following measurements:

    Size 2: 54 x 27 cm (21″ x 10$\frac{1}{2}$″)

    Size 3: 56 x 28 cm (22″ x 11″)

    Size 4: 56 x 29 cm (22″ x 11$\frac{1}{2}$″)

    Size 5: 57 x 30 cm (22$\frac{1}{2}$″ x 12″)

    Size 6: 58 x 30 cm (23″ x 12$\frac{1}{2}$″)

- Cut out two lower frill strips for each size to the following measurements:

    Sizes 2, 3 and 4: 12 x 90 cm (5″ x 36″)

    Size 5: 12 x 95 cm (5″ x 37$\frac{1}{2}$″)

    Size 6: 12 x 100 cm (5″ x 39″)

- Trace off patterns for front and back yokes and sleeve from pattern sheet. Cut out two back yoke pieces, and a strip of fabric 20 x 7.5 cm (8″ x 3″) for continuous band. Cut out three pieces of fabric, large enough to comfortably fit the sleeves and front yoke. These fabric pieces will be stitched with trimming prior to the pattern pieces being cut out. Refer to the techniques for *Joining straight edged insertion to straight edged insertion; Joining a straight lace edge to entredeux; Joining entredeux to flat fabric: Method 1; and Twin needle pin tucks.*

- Find the centre of a sleeve fabric panel. Working from the centre of the panel towards an outer edge, stitch a centred row of insertion lace, then, in order, follow it with parallel rows of beading, entredeux, five twin needle pin tucks, entredeux, a space of 4 cm (1$\frac{1}{2}$″), entredeux, five more twin needle pin tucks, another row of entredeux. Repeat this on the opposite side of centre insertion. Make two panels of identical design. Starch and press these panels. Centre the sleeves on the panels and cut out short sleeves.

- Find the centre of the front yoke panel. Working from the centre of the panel, stitch a centred row of insertion lace, then in order, follow it with parallel rows of beading, entredeux, five twin needle pin tucks, a final row of entredeux. Repeat this trimming on the remaining side of the centred insertion lace. Centre yoke pattern on the panel and cut out.

- Refer to techniques for seam finishes, and use the one of your choice.

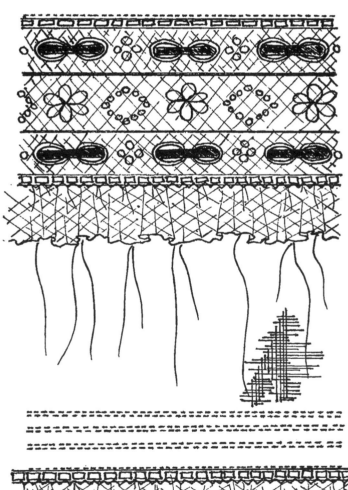

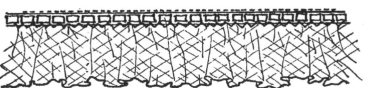

The lacy hem band on 'Phoebe'

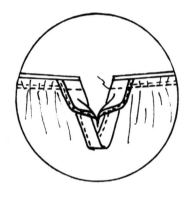

- Join front yoke to back yokes at shoulders.

- Stitch entredeux around armhole, clipping fabric edges for ease. Do not trim off remaining entredeux edge.

- Gather sleeve cap and stitch sleeve to entredeux extension. See technique *Applying entredeux to gathered fabric.*

- Measure upper arm or below elbow and gather lower edge of sleeve to a little more than this measurement, for ease. Apply entredeux to this edge, following the technique used for the sleeve cap. Then add three rows of beading to the entredeux, followed by another row of entredeux with the outer edge untrimmed. Cut a fabric sleeve frill to be $1^1/_2$ times the measurement of the lace band and approximately 5 cm (2") deep, and gather along one long edge. Apply this to the untrimmed entredeux, also using the method in the previous step for the sleeve cap, omitting, at this stage, the holding stitch. Hand gather some edging lace and butt this to the last row of entredeux, over the gathers of the sleeve frill. zigzag this to the entredeux, attaching the lace and holding down the frill gathers at the same time. Add a row of entredeux to the sleeve edge, then add a final row of lace edging to the trimmed entredeux.

- Align the edges of the sleeves and underarm of the front and back bodices and seam together using a French seam.

- Apply untrimmed entredeux to the lower edge of the bodice, extending it to the edge of the back facings.

- Make a 9 cm ($3^1/_2$") split down from the centre top of one skirt panel. Apply a continuous band here. Refer to the technique for *Continuous bands.* Gather the top edges of the skirts.

- Join one side seam in the skirt panels only. Check again for length against the bodice, before starting to stitch in the lacy hem band. Trim away fabric that is not necessary for length from the ungathered skirt edge.

- At the ungathered skirt edge, start with entredeux, add a row of beading, then insertion, then beading, followed by untrimmed entredeux. Seam together one short end of the skirt frill panels only and gather one long edge. Align the frill and skirt seams and stitch gathered frill to entredeux. Hand gather some edging lace and apply below entredeux, as you did for the sleeve frill.

- Check the length of the frill again. When satisfied, add a row of entredeux to the frill edge, then a final row of lace edging to the trimmed entredeux. Add three rows of twin needle tucks above the entredeux.

- Stitch the remaining side seam of the skirt closed, including frill.

- Apply the upper gathered edge of the skirt to the entredeux on the bodice edge, being sure to refer to the illustrations of the *Continuous band*.

- Finish neckline using technique *Finishing a neckline with entredeux and gathered lace*, being sure to extend the trim over the back facings.

- Fold back the back facings and hand sew in place. Make 4 buttonholes on the back facing, and stitch on corresponding buttons.

Phoebe
(Floral version under Pinafore)
See pattern outline on pattern sheet

Refer to the previous version of Phoebe for instructions and fabric quantities. Note that no lace is used on this version, and you should ignore any references to lace embellishment. This dress has deliberately been left unadorned as the pinafore is lavishly trimmed with lace, which complements the pretty Tana Lawn floral fabric. The variations I've made in this version are as follows. Cut dress bodice and sleeves from the pattern pieces on the pattern sheet. You need two backs, one front and two sleeves. Check the lengths given for skirt pieces as the lower frill has been eliminated. The sleeve has been left long, and finished with a continuous band at the split.

Cut fabric strip for this continuous band, as instructed for the centre back opening in the pink lacy version. The neckline is trimmed with a self fabric ruffle, that has its raw edges bound to the neckline. The back opening remains the same, with a turn-back facing and buttons.

Phoebe's Pinafore
See pattern outline on pattern sheet

Cut the pattern pieces from the pattern sheet as directed. You need four backs (two act as self facings), two fronts (again, one acts as a facing) and two armhole ruffle strips. Cut the skirt length as desired, having one full width of 90 cm (36") or 115 cm (45") fabric each for the front and the back. You will need to consider the fabric length needed if you trim the skirt with a band of pleats, a ruffle, or an inset fancy lacy band. Split the back piece in half to give a back opening.

MATERIALS

- 115 cm (45") wide fabric:

    Size 2: 2 m (2$\frac{1}{8}$ yds)

    Size 3 and 4: 2.3 m ((2$\frac{1}{2}$ yds)

    Size 5: 2.4 m (2$\frac{1}{2}$ yds)

    Size 6 2.6 m (2$\frac{3}{4}$ yds)

- Four buttons for back closure

- Laces as desired for trim

METHOD
(1.5 cm ($\frac{5}{8}$") seams allowed)

- Stitch three row of insertion lace down the centre front yoke. Stitch two on each side in a diagonal crisscross pattern, following the technique *Stitching straight edged lace to fabric then cutting away fabric from beneath.*

- Stitch front and back yokes together at shoulders. The trimmed set are the front and back; the remaining set is the facing.

- Trim straight edge of sleeve ruffles with lace as de-

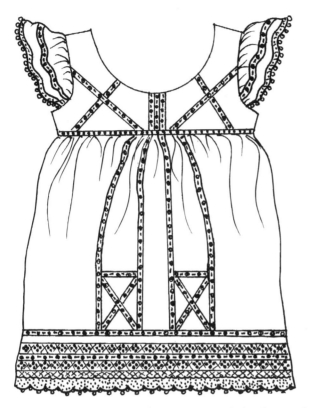

Lace placement on Phoebe's pinafore

sired, or use techniques for *Join straight lace edge to fabric* and stitch a strip of insertion in from the edge using the front yoke technique.

- Gather curved edge of ruffles, then, with right sides facing and raw edges matching, stitch to armholes of trimmed front and back between markings.

- Match the raw edges of the facing with front and back, right sides facings and align shoulder seams, then stitch following stitch line for ruffle around the armholes. Push the ruffles away and stitch up the backs and around the neckline. Clip seams for ease and trim to 6 mm (1/4″). Don't stitch underarm seams.

- Turn to right side by pulling backs through shoulders and out at front. Press neatly.

- Finish underarm seams with a French seam. Join the skirt sections at the side seams using French seams.

- I have added several bands of insertion to the skirt, forming panels enclosing a crisscross of lace using the technique *Stitching straight edged lace to fabric then cutting away fabric from beneath*. See illustration. The lower skirt is trimmed with a fancy band of joined

insertion laces, finished with a row of edging. See techniques for *Joining straight edged insertion lace to straight edged insertion.*

- Turn the back skirt edges under 1 cm ($\frac{1}{2}$"), trim to 6 mm ($\frac{1}{4}$"), then fold again 2 cm (1"). Stitch along inner fold.

- With right sides facing and raw edges matching, pin, then stitch the skirt to the front and back, keeping facing layer free, and matching side seams. Position folded back edges of skirt at seam in back bodices.

- Trim away skirt and yoke seam allowance to be 8 mm ($\frac{3}{8}$") wide, then fold under raw edges of facing 1.5 cm ($\frac{5}{8}$") and press. Trim facing allowance back to 8 mm ($\frac{3}{8}$"). Hand sew the folded facing edge to the stitching for the skirt.

- Mark and make four buttonholes in the back bodice overlap, and sew buttons to corresponding positions in remaining overlap.

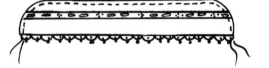

Armhole ruffles with edging, insertion and gathers in place

Alice

I have trimmed the collar and skirt points with small blue grub roses, then used a pale blue satin ribbon for a sash. Seam allowances are 1.5 cm ($^5/_8$″).

MATERIALS

- 115 cm (45″) wide fabric

  Sizes 4 and 5 – 2.20m ($2^3/_8$ yds)

- Lace and ribbons as desired

- 7 buttons for back closure

Back view of Alice's collar

METHOD

- Trace off pattern from pattern sheet and cut out two sleeves, one front and two backs, collar front and back, front and back neckline facings.

- 1.5 cm ($^5/_8$″) seams are allowed, except where otherwise specified.

- Cut 2 upper and 2 lower skirt panels to the following measurements:

Upper skirt panel:

   71 x 18 cm (28″ x 7″)

Lower skirt panel:

   71 x 30 cm (28″ x 12″)

- If tucks are to be used on the front, cut out a panel of fabric wide enough to allow for six 1 cm (1/2") tucks in width, mark and sew the tucks, following the technique *Tucks*, then cut out the bodice front.

- Join the collar front to the backs at shoulders. Do not overcast the seam. Trim the seam allowance to 6 mm (1/4") and press the seam flat.

- Find and press a crease at the centre front of the collar, then pin a length of starched insertion lace down this line. Pin other lengths over the shoulder seams. Pin other strips between these rows and parallel to them, and another between the centre back line and the shoulders. Stitch these using the technique *Stitching straight edged lace to fabric then cutting away fabric from beneath*.

- Taking a continuous length of starched lace, pin lace length down the back opening, so that the outside edge of lace matches centre back line, around edge of collar, angling lace at points and back up remaining back edge. Stitch lace to collar using techniques *Joining a straight lace edge to fabric* and *Sewing flat lace to an angle that is not 90 degrees*. Butt another row of insertion lace up to the outside row and stitch them together using narrow zigzag. zigzag over the fold in the angles and cut away excess lace from beneath.

- Stitch 18 cm (7") lengths of insertion lace down the front from the shoulder seams, approximately 4 cm (1 1/2") in from the armhole. End these rows of lace with a point, as instructed in the technique *Stitching straight edged lace to fabric and cutting away fabric from beneath*.

- Press a crease down the centre of the sleeves and use this as a guide to centre and stitch a strip of starched insertion lace.Add strips either side (not butted) that are 23 cm (9") long, ending in points. Add more strips on the outside of these that are 15 cm (6") long, also ending in points. Cut away fabric underneath.

- Join front bodice to back bodices at shoulders.

- Gather the sleeve cap and stitch the sleeve into the armhole.

- Pin, then stitch, continuous seams from cuffs to waist.

- Apply the continuous bands in each sleeve, referring to the technique *Continuous bands.*

- Check the length of the cuffs and shorten if necessary. Check the wrist measurement and add 2 cm (1") for ease.

- Gather the sleeve lower edges and apply entredeux, equal to the wrist measurement plus ease, referring to technique for *Applying entredeux to gathered fabric.*

- Place one long edge of the cuff against the entredeux extension, right sides facing, and stitch. Press the remaining long cuff edge in 1.5 cm ($^5/_8$").

- Fold the cuff in half lengthways to have right sides facing and short ends matching and stitch across short ends. Turn cuff out, with the folded edge inside. Align the folded edge with cuff stitching and hand sew the edge in place.

- Pin the collar around the neckline on the right side. Stitch together the front and back facings at shoulders, and press open the seams. Fold the back facings along fold lines to the right side (they will cover the edge of the collar). Place the neck facing, right sides facing, onto the collar, matching neckline edges. Stitch around entire neckline. Trim to layer the seam allowances and reduce bulk, then clip the seam allowances for ease. Turn neck facing and back facings in, and press. Hand sew the facing to the shoulder seams to hold facing in place.

- Overlap the back openings and baste across the lower edge to hold.

- Join the side seams of the upper and lower skirts.

- With side seams at the side, fold the upper skirt into half, then half again. Mark up the folded edges 7 cm (3"). Draw down from these points to the centre of the lower edge, creating a point. Cut along these lines. Unfold the upper skirt and you will find it zigzagged, with four points each in the front and back. Practise on paper first if you're uncertain.

- Trim the edge of the zigzags with two rows of insertion lace, in the same way as you stitched the lace to the collar's edge. At the upper point in the zigzagged trim stitch 7 cm (3") strips of insertion lace down

from the upper raw edge, ending in points, as in the trim of the collar and sleeves.

- Cut off a 10 cm (4″) strip from around the lower edge of the under skirt. Rejoin it to the skirt, after inserting entredeux, following the technique *Inserting entredeux into fabric, with hem.*

- Place the skirts together, with the under skirt beneath the trimmed upper skirt and align upper raw edges and side seams. Gather along top edges.

- With right sides facing and raw edges and side seams matching, pin, then stitch the gathered skirt edges to the lower edge of the bodice.

- Make buttonholes in the back opening and cuffs, then stitch on buttons.

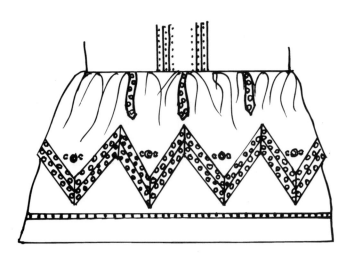

Alice's skirt and overskirt

Lucy the heirloom doll
Patterns illustrated on pattern sheet

Dress this whimsical doll in matching dress, pantaloons and a Pilgrim bonnet. She's quite a picture, right down to her matching shoes! Add the lace trim as you wish, for dolls' dresses provide great opportunities for using up scraps of lace. Seam allowances are 1 cm (½") throughout, and Lucy stands around 50 cm (20") high when complete.

MATERIALS

- 1·10 m (3'8") of 90 cm (36") wide cotton voile (I used a Liberty fabric)

- Lace trim as desired (see note below)

- Scrap of silk ribbon for neck bow

- 50 cm (20") of 115 cm (45") wide off-white cotton fabric for doll, Polyester stuffing for doll

- Elastic for pantaloons

- Three small press studs for back closure

- Interfacing for the bonnet brim

Note on laces used: I have used edging, beading, wide entredeux and insertion on the dress, edging on the bonnet, and beading and edging on the pantaloons. Be sure to stitch curves and tight corners on the doll twice for strength, and to clip into seam allowances at curves for ease before turning the doll to the right side.

Doll

METHOD

- Trace off the pattern pieces from the pattern sheet and cut out as instructed. Cut two head/arm/torso pieces and four legs from off-white fabric. Cut four shoe pieces from cotton voile.

- Baste wrong side of shoe pieces to right side of legs, matching lower raw edges. Satin stitch over upper edge of shoes, fastening them to the legs.

- Place the legs in pairs, right sides facing and raw edges matching. Stitch around long sides and feet, leaving an opening for stuffing at the calf and leaving the top straight edge open. Turn legs to right side and fold, then baste, to align the seams at the centre.

- Place torso pieces together, right sides facing and raw edges matching. Stitch around from hips, through head and down to hips again, leaving an opening for stuffing below an underarm and leaving lower torso edge open. Take care to shape the thumb areas well. Turn body to right side and stuff the arms, filling up to about 2 cm (1″) away from the shoulder stitching line. Stitch along these lines, through all thicknesses.

- Place the legs, right sides facing, onto the lower torso front edge, matching raw edges. Be sure you have them facing the right way – when Lucy is standing her toes should face the front! Stitch legs to torso front, leaving torso back free. Stuff the body and legs. Hand sew openings in legs closed. You may need to ease in some fullness when hand sewing the lower back torso closed, and add more stuffing just before stitching is completed.

Dress, pantaloons and bonnet

METHOD

- Trace off pattern pieces from pattern sheet and cut out as instructed. Cut one front, two backs, two sleeves, one bonnet, one brim and two pantaloons.

- Trim the short frill ends using a glass to shape the curve (see illustration).

- Cut two skirt pieces 16 cm x 70 cm (6½″ x 27″) and two shoulder frills 7 cm x 40 cm (2¾″ x 16″) from cotton voile.

- Join one side seam of the skirt using a French seam. Press the skirt into 6 or 7 divisions. Using these creases, apply insertion to the fabric in zigzags, folding the lace at the top of each point and at the hem, revealing the wrong side of the lace, to continue the pattern. Use the technique *Stitching straight edged lace to fabric, then cutting away the fabric from beneath.* Trim

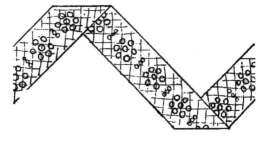

Lace on lucy's skirt

the hem with two rows of beading and one of edging lace. Finish the remaining side seam with a French seam.

- Find the centre back and cut down 5 cm (2") to make a back opening. Edge this opening with edging lace, using the technique *Joining a straight lace edge to fabric.*

- Stitch beading and edging laces down bodice centre front using the technique *Joining a straight lace edge to a straight lace edge.* Stitch edging lace to neckline/shoulder edges of bodice fronts and backs, and press inside. Stitch beading and edging down the sleeve centres, and to the long straight edge of the frills, cutting away fabric from beneath beading. Stitch beading and edging to lower edges of pantaloons. Stitch edging around curved edge of bonnet.

- Measure Lucy's wrists loosely and gather the sleeve lower edges, then trim with entredeux, using the technique *Applying entredeux to gathered fabric.* Trim away the remaining edge of entredeux and apply edging. Gather the centred frill strips and sleeve caps along raw edges (frills are much fuller than sleeve caps) and baste frills to sleeve caps.

- Butt the bodice front and backs together at the neckline. Take a few holding stitches to secure the pieces together at the shoulders. Stitch the frill trimmed sleeves into the armholes. Stitch the underarm and bodice sides in a continuous seam.

- Gather the upper edge of skirt and join it to the lower bodice edge from centre back line to centre back line, noting back fold-in facings and pushing the lace from the skirt opening to either side. Fold back the facings and hand sew in place. Stitch on press studs.

- Stitch edging lace 1 cm (3/8") in from one long raw edge of interfaced bonnet brim. Fold brim to have wrong sides facing and long edges matching, then stitch short ends, turn, press. Gather straight edge of bonnet and stitch to trimmed edge of brim, having right sides facing and raw edges even. Turn in remaining raw edge of brim and hand sew to stitching. This will enclose the gathered bonnet edge. Make two parallel rows of gathering stitch 2 cm (3/4") in on the curved edge of bonnet. Draw up these threads and thread onto a needle. Try bonnet on Lucy and adjust

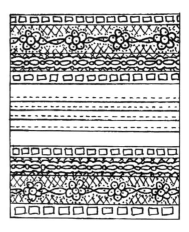

A suggestion for a lacy hem band in projects

gathers, then stitch, with ends of gathering threads, through brim seam to Lucy's head to secure.

- Place pantaloons together, right sides facing and edges even. Stitch curved crotch seams. Fold pantaloons to align crotch seams in centre. Stitch inner leg seams from ankle to ankle. Fold over waist edge 3 mm (1/8") then again 1 cm (1/2") and stitch casing, leaving opening for elastic insertion. Insert elastic, try on Lucy and adjust, hand stitch to secure elastic ends.

- Tie small bow from silk ribbon and stitch to centre front neckline, then add blusher to her cheeks.

Credits

Thank you to Kate McEwan from the Kate McEwan Sewing Centre in Chatswood, Sydney for heirloom sewing reference material, laces and the christening gown. Kate runs classes in heirloom sewing at her shop. Thank you Liberty Fabrics for the beautiful florals and small prints used throughout the book; to Ray Toby Fabrics in Sydney for the plain cotton voiles in pastel colours; and to Grosvenor Antiques, Lindfield, Sydney for the fabric lined decoupaged box on the cover. Thank you Bernina for your superb sewing machines – they're a pleasure to use.

For information about craft kits and materials available from Tonia Todman, please write to:

Tonia Todman Craft Kits
PO Box 12
Balmain NSW 2041